G'Day!
Welcome to the Animal Hospital Annual. I know that you love animals as much as I do. They give so much love and ask nothing in return. But they do depend on us to look after them. Whether you care for a cat or a mouse, you'll find lots ot tips in this book for being a better pet owner. Plus, there are lots of stories from your favourite programme, puzzles, and a great animal tale.
Keep on Caring.

 Rolf

CONTENTS

Editor Claire Comins
Art Editor Maria Goodspeed
Sub Editor Sarah Armstrong-Prior
Written by Claire Comins, Sarah Armstrong-Prior

With special thanks to Pippa Bush and all at the RSPCA, and everyone on the BBC Animal Hospital team.

All photography from **BBC** Worldwide/ Richard Kendal or taken from
BBC Animal Hospital, except:
p2-3, p8-9, p14-16, p28, p34-35, p40-41, p49, p54, p64 all Bruce Coleman
p16 NCDL
p20, p29, p42 FLPA
p46-47 Photographs from **BBC Girltalk** magazine
p48 Ardea
p55 NHPA

Illustrations by:
p12-13 Jane Andrews
p17, p44-45, p60-61 Kate Shannon
p22-26 Rachel B Stevens
p43 Carole Daniel/**BBC Smart** magazine

ROLF HARRIS

Animal Hospital has won many awards – what's the key to its success?
It shows, as realistically as possible, what actually goes on in a veterinary hospital clinic and operating theatre. The vets, owners and animals are all real, as are the situations! Nobody is writing a script for the owners or vets to say. I try to get explanations for things that may seem complex, or make sure the vet translates medical terms so that ordinary people can understand them. It's a wonderful on-going excitement: what is going to happen to that dog or cat next week?

Why do you love working on it?
I feel I can comfort worried owners and also calm nervous pets. And most people know me when they come in and feel at ease with me – almost as if I am an old friend. This takes away a lot of their tension. It's great to be able to let viewers know about pet care and the simple checks you can make on your pet's health.

How old were you when you got your first pet and what was it?
The first cat I can remember was 'Pussy', a very imaginative name! We got her when I was almost three and when I left to come to England she was still around, and aged 19. I think owning pets has given me a very good insight into what the owners are going through when their animal is ill or injured.

What's the most valuable lesson you've learnt about owning pets?
To get your pet to see a vet as soon as you notice a lump or bump, or any completely new and unusual behaviour. You may be able to catch a problem and get it fixed before it grows to life-threatening proportions. Your dog or cat can't tell you – you have to be observant. And don't wait over a weekend – it may be too late for your pet. There are always emergency clinics you can go to.

What are the saddest moments on Animal Hospital?
It's very sad when owners bring in unvaccinated dogs and realise they have parvo virus and may very quickly die. Their realisation that they could have prevented this crisis is heartbreaking.

What are the best?
The best moments are when an animal is at death's door, through a road traffic accident or cruelty or neglect, or through some life-threatening disease, and the expertise of the vets and nurses gives them a fighting chance. The body then just miraculously heals, and the animal bounces out again as its old self. They are great moments, watching owners and their pets joyfully reunited.

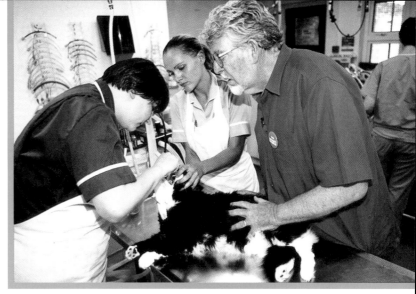

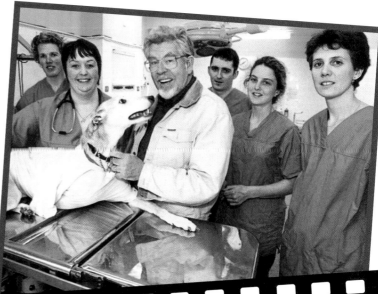

What do you feel is the most important part of the work the RSPCA does?
The RSPCA's work is two-fold – firstly, tracking down and stopping cruelty to animals and secondly providing care for animals, both domestic pets and wildlife.
Hopefully, by their example, they are educating a lot of people and changing attitudes about animals for the better.

It's been shown that animals can help people recover from illness – why do you think this is?
I think it is the calming effect of stroking a living, breathing and loving creature. It has no words to give you; the doctors and nurses do that. The animal just gives you unconditional love – and that heals.

If you could have one wish regarding animal welfare, what would it be?
My one wish would be that people became aware of the fact that animals have feelings just as we have, and that giving them love and kindness and looking after their needs will give you a friend that will love you unconditionally throughout its relatively short life.

7

Rabbits

Pet care

● As rabbits are sociable animals, the RSPCA recommends you keep two pet bunnies as company for eachother. Don't forget to get your bunnies neutered or you could either have more company than you had planned, or some nasty fights between the bullying boys!

● Rabbits can live for five to ten years and need daily care – that's a lot of cleaning of smelly living areas!

● Rabbits are herbivores. Among their favourite foods are: grass, hay, cabbage, broccoli, carrots and apples (but not too many). Along with plenty of fresh water to drink, they need a small portion of fibre-rich pellets to provide them with a balanced diet.

● Inspect and groom your rabbit daily with a firm brush to keep its coat healthy, clean and flea free. This is a perfect opportunity for 'quality time'!

What do you get if you cross a flea with a rabbit?

Bug's bunny!

What are bunnies best at?

Rabbiting on!

Amazing facts

● A female rabbit can have up to seven litters a year, with between three and twelve babies in each – and your mum thinks she's busy!

● As a rabbit's eyes are on the side of its head, it can almost see behind itself without turning.

● Tame rabbits were originally bred from the wild in Europe, so domestic and common European rabbits belong to the same species

called 'Oryctologus cuniculus.' Today there are over 55 different breeds of rabbits.

● The Champagne D'Argent is the only domestic breed that changes colour. The rabbits are born black and change to a dull silver as they grow.

● In the wild a group of rabbits (called a herd) lives in a warren. A male rabbit is called a buck and a female rabbit is called a doe.

Cats in a FIX!

Cats are good at getting into a tight spot, as RSPCA teams know too well. Here are some of the greatest rescue stories that the Animal Hospital team have caught on film.

STUCK!

Lewis the cat had been up on the roof all night, wailing and obviously stuck. So when the RSPCA officer came

to help his owner rescue him, he lost no time enlisting the help of the local fire brigade and their long ladder. But just as the fireman climbed up to reach him, Lewis grew scared and hid behind a chimney stack. After a lot of gentle coaxing, the fireman brought him safely down to his relieved owner – who gave Lewis a big cuddle.

DRIP!

Cats love climbing trees, but what about ladders? RSPCA Inspector Simon Davies' ladder wasn't long enough to reach the bottom of this London canal, so he couldn't climb down to reach the cat who'd fallen in the water. Instead, all he and Animal Collection Officer Christine Graham could do was dangle the ladder and hope the cat would claw up to saftey. After a few splashy moments it did, and immediatly shot off (hopefully back home)!

UPSET

'I've got him, but he's a bit upset,' said RSPCA Inspector John Gibson as he finally managed to get Tim out from under his new owner's shed. It had been a long struggle to rescue the cat, who had been chased out of his new home by the owner's other cat only a day and a half after arriving. As Animal Collection Officer Sue Briggs explained, 'He doesn't know where he is, he doesn't know how to get home, and he's very, very scared.' John had been called in because he had an extra-long grasper to reach under to the back of the shed – and it worked. 'Oh thank you so much,' said owner Nicola Axam when she saw her new cat again. Nicola was advised to keep him indoors for three to four weeks to stop a similar thing happening again.

MECHANIC!

RSPCA officers are called out to rescue cats from all kinds of places – but from a car? It might sound silly, but Madeline McIntyre's one-eyed cat Emma hates travelling so much that she'd got out of her box in the car on the way to the RSPCA Putney Hospital and, in Madeline's words, was 'going beserk!' Inspector Dermott Murphy soon got Emma into the cage and down to the hospital where she was treated for the original thing she came for – fleas.

TOO FAR

'Oh! Complete relief!' said Judy Harrison when she was reunited with her cat, Tod, who had climbed a bit too far up a tree and got stuck. Judy had hardly slept all night worrying about him, so was more than happy to stand out in the rain and watch the rescue with Animal Hospital presenter Edwina Silver. The fire fighter climbed up a 15-metre ladder to within arm's reach of Tod, only to see him move even further along the branch! Eventually, though, he got hold of him and carried him down to Judy who took Tod indoors for food, sleep, and more food!

British woods are teeming with wildlife in late spring. Unmuddle the names of the animals listed, then see how many you can spot in this early evening scene.

relsquir _____ 4

rede _____ 3

gerbad _____ 1

xof _____ 1

teflybutr _____ 3

pecwoodker _____ 2

gofr _____ 5

twen _____ 1

gehoghed _____ 2

flyondrag _____ 1

wol _____ 1

Turn to page 58 to see if you are right!

Dogs

Pet care

● Friend for life! Dogs can live for ten years or more and require a lot of daily care and attention. In return they make loyal and fun-loving friends.

● Being a dog is thirsty work! They need clean, fresh drinking water available at all times.

● As you can probably guess, the amount of food your pet dog needs varies according to their size! *All* dogs need a balanced diet, which usually means a mixture of special dried foods or biscuits and some meat (tinned or fresh).

● An occasional treat of a special chew will help keep your dog's teeth and gums healthy and prevent that dreaded smelly dog breath!

● Dogs get bored easily and have lots of energy (whatever their size) so they need regular exercise. This means two walks a day to places where they can safely be let off the lead to run and play.

● Follow my lead! All dogs must be taught to walk with a collar and lead as soon as possible. They need to respond to their names and the command 'no.' 'sit', 'stay', 'come' and 'heel' follow later!

● Male dogs tend to be more independent, more tricky to train and control then females, and may tend to fight with other dogs and worry other animals like cats and sheep. Dog-training schools can help you deal with problems like these.

● Female dogs are naturally more loving than males but can cost more to buy and need to be neutered as some can have litters every six months.

● The longer a dog's coat is, the more grooming (brushing and bathing) he or she needs. Neglect can lead to painful and expensive vet visits.

● All dogs need vaccinations as puppies, regular worming and usually de-fleaing, too (see page 52).

What dog loves to take bubble baths?

A shampoodle!

Dogs

What kind of dog does a vampire prefer? A bloodhound!

What is the dog's favourite city? New Yorkie!

Amazing facts!

● On August 11th, 1999, the largest dog biscuit in the world measured in at 2.35m long, 57cm wide and 2.54cm thick. It was made in Minneapolis (USA). What a mouthful!

● From hungry to heavy… Kell, an English Mastiff bitch (female) is the heaviest living dog. Recorded on 18 August 1999 in Loughborough, Kell weighed a massive 130 kilograms.

● The Old English Mastiff and the St Bernard are the heaviest breeds of domestic dogs, with males of both breeds regularly weighing between 77 and 91 kilograms.

● The Basenji is the only breed of dog that cannot bark. It is a small, short-haired, hunting dog from Africa and the breed dates back to the days of the Pharaohs and ancient Egypt. Although they are naturally barkless, they are not mute and make other sounds common to all dogs.

● The oldest documented dog was an Australian cattle dog called Bluey. Incredibly, Bluey lived to the great old age of 29 years and five months!

● In Greek mythology, Argos, Ulysses' hunting dog, was the only creature to recognise the hero when he returned home disguised as a beggar after nearly 20 years of adventures.

● Cruft's Dog Show is over 100 years old. It is named after its founder, Charles Cruft, and the first show was held in London in 1891. In 1948 the current organisers, the Kennel Club, took the event over.

Draw a dog

1. Draw two ovals for a basic outline.
2. Add lines for the ears, tail and legs.
3. Fill out the shapes ready to colour in.

One of the best things about being a presenter on Animal Hospital is meeting the people who dedicate their lives to animals. Edwina Silver reports on a very special lady who runs a Donkey Sanctuary in Devon

Now, where did you get that hat?

A WELCOME HOME

WITH EDWINA SILVER

Running an animal sanctuary takes patience and Elisabeth Svendsen, who runs the Donkey Sanctuary in Sidmouth, Devon, has balefuls of it. She has worked at the sanctuary nearly every day for 30 years. The RSPCA regularly refers cases of homeless donkeys to the sanctuary, but Elisabeth's first one was rescued from a beach.

'It was so weak, I had to feed it with a glucose drip,' she told me. 'From then on, I decided I was just going to rescue donkeys.'

Over the years, she has cared for over 8,300 donkeys. They have not all been mistreated. I met Butch, whose owner, Jack, brought him to the sanctuary when he felt too old to care for

Little Donkey, Little Donkey.

Elisabeth Svendsen introduces Edwina to Butch

him. Jack used to come on holiday nearby to visit Butch and both were very happy. But when Jack died, Butch lost weight. Elisabeth had the brainwave of putting an ad in the paper for elderly gentlemen. She got in four 'Butchsitters' and Butch is back to his normal self.

Elisabeth's main concern is to give the donkeys a good quality of life, but that doesn't mean the donkeys can't help others. One donkey goes out to cheer up people in a retirement home, special needs children come for riding lessons, and when I was at the sanctuary, a primary school put on their nativity play. Rhodri and I had fun creating the setting, but best of all was the performance. And there was no question as to how Mary would arrive — on a donkey, of course!

It's free to visit The Donkey Sanctuary. Call 01395 578222 for details.

SUPER SNAPS!

Here's a quick look at some of the programme's highlights.

Birds of a feather... perch together!

When you're as precious as these parrots, *under cover* is the only way to travel...

'You did say you didn't mind heights, didn't you?' says Edwina to a firefighter who'd disappeared up a tree after a cat.

Ready, very steady... and Tessa's nearly got this dog's collar from out of his stomach.

Stick your left paw out... even puppies can have acupuncture.

Guinea pigs

Pet care

● Domesticated guinea pigs (called cavies) have a typical lifespan of four to seven years.

● Because they are sociable animals and live in family groups in the wild, the RSPCA recommends that more than one pet guinea pig is kept, for companionship. A good tip is to choose two young litter mates of the same sex, or a father and son, or a mother and daughter.

● Guinea pigs are vegetarians and can be fussy eaters! They should be fed twice a day on a mixture of special guinea pig food (from a pet shop), meadow hay, cereal and washed fresh fruit and green vegetables (but not lettuce). They need a supply of drinking water and a gnawing block to wear down long teeth.

● Pet guinea pigs need daily exercise in a safe, grassy area or an indoor run in cold weather.

● A guinea pig can be kept indoors or out, but its waterproof home should always be placed out of direct sunlight and strong winds or draughts.

Amazing facts!

● Domesticated guinea pigs are descended from the wild guinea pigs (*Cavia aperea*) of Peru and Brazil, where they are used as a source of food.

● Guinea pigs are rodents. A female guinea pig is called a sow and a male is a boar. Unlike most rodents, guinea pigs can see in colour.

● Folk doctors in the Andes use guinea pigs to detect sickness. They believe that when the rodent is pressed against an ill person, it will squeak if it is near the source of the disease!

● Guinea pigs can have up to five litters a year of one to four babies, but in 1972 a litter of 12 guinea pigs was recorded!

● Guinea pigs were domesticated by the Incas around 500 years ago and were brought over to Europe by the Spaniards over 400 years ago.

GOLDEN OPPO

Read this story about adopting a pet from an RSPCA centre. Then try to answer the questions at the end!

Katie and Tom's mum, Sue, wasn't too keen on the idea of them getting a dog at first. "You can't

even keep your rooms tidy, let alone keep a pet!" she told them whenever they asked. But the more Sue thought about it, the more she warmed to the idea.

"But, Mum, you always say we're spending too much time indoors," Katie would argue. "Yeah," agreed Tom. "If we had a dog, we would have to exercise it at least twice a day," he reasoned. "And play with it," Katie added.

Perhaps having a dog wouldn't be such a bad idea, she thought. Katie and Tom loved animals, they did get bored easily and they were actually agreeing on something for a change – quite something as they usually fought the whole time.

"OK. Here's the deal," she finally agreed. "If you can keep your rooms tidy, do all of your homework, go outdoors to play twice a day and be home in time for tea over the next two weeks, we'll go and investigate at the RSPCA centre."

Over the next two weeks, Katie and Tom kept their word and Sue was amazed when she realised they had hardly bickered, either. Then, one day, Katie and Tom came home for tea looking extremely pleased with themselves.

"OK, what have you two been up to? You look like the cats who got the cream – and I know this isn't your favourite supper, so something is definitely up!" said their mum suspiciously, over tea.

Katie and Tom grinned at each other, nodded, and then Tom jumped up from the table and left the room. "Where do you think you're going? You haven't finished yet," Sue called out after him. "You'll see, Mum," Katie laughed.

When Tom returned, Sue was even more curious. Tom was laden down with books – and he'd never exactly been fond of studying at the best of times.

"We've been to the library," said Katie. "We thought it would be a good idea to find out all about dogs," she explained. "You know, about the different breeds and how to look after them and stuff," volunteered Tom.

"Well, I have to say I'm gobsmacked!" laughed Sue. "You two have really thought about this, haven't you?" she said. So go on, tell me what you've learnt."

Tom and Katie took turns telling their mum all about what sort of care different dogs needed. "We did want one of those great big fluffy dogs like on the Dulux advert, but then we found out that the long-haired breeds need more grooming. And then we thought about a puppy, but puppies have to be house trained and all sorts," explained Katie.

"And obviously if we lived in a smaller house with a tiny garden, a big dog wouldn't have enough space," said Tom, smugly. "But our garden isn't too small for, say, a medium-sized dog."

"I'm impressed," said Sue. "And

RTUNITY!

not just because you've been down the library – although that is a pretty amazing feat coming from you two," she beamed. "Over the past two weeks you have done everything I asked and more. So now it's time for me to keep my side of the bargain. Who fancies going to find out more about this down at the RSPCA centre tomorrow?" she asked, knowing what their answer would be. "Yeah! Oh can we?" they called together.

The next day was Saturday. Tom and Katie woke up pretty early and soon made it clear to Sue that she wasn't going to get a lie-in, either. "Morning, Mum!" said Tom.

Sue opened her eyes to see Tom and Katie stood by her bed, with Katie holding a tray with breakfast on it. "We thought you might be hungry, so we made you breakfast," said Katie.

Sue looked at the tray, looked at her clock, and groaned. "It's only seven o'clock, guys. The RSPCA centre doesn't even open until ten!"

Katie, Tom and their mum arrived at the RSPCA centre at ten on the dot. "You look like some pretty keen customers," said the lady at the desk. "I've just this minute opened up! My name's Jackie, I'm a volunteer here. How can I help you?" she asked.

"We've come to adopt a dog!" announced Tom, before their mum had even had a chance to speak. "Hmm, yes. Well, it's not quite that straightforward,

is it?" said Sue.

"You're right," said Jackie kindly, looking at Tom and Katie. "Not many people realise this, but before you can take an animal home from here, you have to be approved," she said. "What do you mean by approved?" quizzed Katie.

"Well, firstly we need to find out why you want an animal and

whether you realise how much work it's going to be. Then we have to work out what sort of animal would suit your family best," explained Jackie.

"Oh," said Tom gloomily, "You mean we can't just pick one?" "I'm afraid not. Remember, we don't want either you or your pet to be unhappy," she added.

Jackie smiled politely at Sue and said, "How about we take it a step at a time? Why don't you start by filling in this form?" "Thank you," said Sue. "That would be great."

Over the next 15 minutes, Jackie explained why the RSPCA needed to ask the questions on the form, while Tom, Katie and Sue filled in their answers. Jackie explained that, at the end of the day, the RSPCA was concerned about the welfare of animals, and this meant making sure that each animal was adopted into the right home. "So what's the next step? Do we get to look at the dogs now?" asked Katie.

"Once we've looked over your

form, a volunteer rehoming visitor will arrange to come and see you at home," said Jackie brightly. "If the home visit goes well, then you can come back and look at the animals we have here."

Katie, Tom and their mum thanked Jackie and drove back home. Sue could see the children were disappointed.

"Don't be sad," said Sue. Jackie told us that with any luck, a rehoming visitor will call round in a few days' time," she offered. "I know," said Tom. "We just weren't expecting it to be so difficult, that's all."

Later that week, Katie heard a knock at the door. "I'll get it!" she shouted excitedly, and ran down to find out whether it was someone from the centre.

"Hello, my name's John, I'm from the RSPCA. I'm your volunteer," he explained. "Oh, hi!" said Katie, shyly. "Mum!" she called. "Come quickly, it's the rehoming man!"

Sue made some coffee for her and John while Tom and Katie showed John round their house and garden. Then they sat down in the living room together and John told Tom, Katie, and their mum all about his job.

"It's my job to see how much space you've got and find out how much time you can spend with a pet. We can talk about the day-to-day needs of different pets and I'll try to answer any questions you might have. Does that sound OK by you?" he grinned.

Sue explained all about the deal with her children, and how Tom and Katie had been to the library and read up on dogs.

"I'm very impressed," John said with a smile. "It sounds like you could create a great home for a dog. Why don't you two tell me what conclusion

you've come to, having read all those books?" he asked.

"We thought a puppy would be too much work, and Mum would hate dog hairs everywhere all the time so we'd like a short-haired one, too," said Tom.

"So we thought we could see if there was a dog at the centre that wasn't too young, hopefully one that had been trained already, but not too old, either," explained Katie. "And as there's a park down the road and we've got quite a large garden, we hoped we might be able to get a fairly big dog, like a Labrador or something," finished Sue.

"Great! That's about all I needed to know. I'm going to report back to the animal home manager now and she'll ring to let you know if the adoption can go ahead," he said as he was leaving.

Later that afternoon, the manager of the RSPCA centre rang to say that everything was

fine and that they were very welcome to pop along and have a look at the dogs waiting for new homes.

The following Wednesday, they went back to the centre. Katie and Tom could hardly contain themselves – they were so excited. "Hello – back already?" said Jackie, as they walked in. "I take it your home visit went well then," she added, smiling. "Yes, it did," said Katie. "Would it be alright if we had a look at some dogs?" asked Sue politely. "Of course! In fact, I think John's about somewhere, I'll see if he can show you around."

Jackie disappeared for a minute and then came back with John, the volunteer who had visited them at home. "Hi. If you're ready, let's go!" grinned Tom.

John showed them about ten dogs that he thought might be suitable. "What about that one?" asked Katie, when she saw a cute, chocolate coloured dog in a kennel they were walking past.

"He's called Frank," John told them. "Frank *seems* pretty quiet, but he's quite a handful – I think you'll love the one I'm going to show you next."

"She's beautiful!" squealed Katie. John had taken them to a kennel at the end of the row, where a yellow Labrador cross stood, wagging her tail as they approached. "I thought you'd like her," said John.

"This lovely lady is called

Goldie. She is very affectionate, smart and she's pretty playful – but not quite the handful that Frank is," grinned John. "When you were telling me about the dog you thought might suit you best, Goldie immediately sprang to mind," he said.

"Can we stroke her?" asked Tom, nervously. "Course you can!" laughed John. "In fact, why don't we put her on a lead and take her outside to the exercise area so you can get to know each other a bit better. What do you think?" he asked, looking at Sue.

"That sounds great, doesn't it, guys?" Sue laughed, as she looked round to see Tom and Katie nearly jumping with excitement.

John took a lead off a hook on the wall, attached it to Goldie's collar and opened the kennel door. "Who wants to say hello first, then?" he asked Tom and Katie. They looked at each other and decided that Katie would stroke Goldie and Tom would hold the lead first.

Goldie seemed as excited to meet them as they were. "Don't let her take you for a walk, Tom!" said John, as Goldie started bounding off with Tom flying behind her, desperately trying to get her to slow down.

"Goldie, heel!" said John sternly and took the lead from Tom. Goldie immediately slowed down to walk at the same pace as John.

Over the next half an hour, John very kindly showed Tom, Katie and Sue how to control Goldie on the lead. Then they took Goldie back inside and went to pick up her folder.

"This is full of information about Goldie and about how to look after her, including what to do if she gets fleas or ticks, for

example," explained John. "I'll need you to fill out another form, like a certificate, to say that you have adopted Goldie. She's already been neutered and we'll update her microchip information on the PetLog database with your address and contact details, and then you can take her home!"

"Thanks, John," said Katie and Tom, after Sue had paid the adoption fee and sorted out all of the paperwork. "Yes, thank you," said their mum.

"Will we see you again?" asked Katie. "I'll tell you what, I'll come back in a month or so's time, to see how you're all getting on," smiled John. "Take care now. Bye!"

Tom and Katie were thrilled with their new friend. "Goldie's the best dog in the world!" said Tom. "Yeah!" agreed Katie. "I know, let's take her to the park. Can we, Mum?" she pleaded. "OK, but you'll have to wait for me – I want to come along, too!" said Sue, laughing.

An hour later Tom, Katie and even Sue were running as fast as they could. "Goldie, come back!" Goldie was so excited to see the park that she had taken off again, leaving the rest of them behind. "Goldie, heel!" shouted Tom, firmly.

"Katie, you're going to have to learn to hold on when she pulls," puffed their mum crossly, as she caught up with Goldie and Tom.

"Unless we all learn how to control Goldie properly, we're all going to be miserable pretty quickly – what if Goldie ran out into the road?" Sue added.

Over the next couple of weeks, Goldie, Katie and Tom took turns wearing each other out and getting each other into big trouble with Mum!

"Who brought Goldie back from the park with muddy paws? Look at my nice, clean floor – ruined!" grumbled their mum one day. The next day, it was a similar story. "Oh, Mum. Tom brought Goldie into my bedroom and they knocked over a glass of water all over my homework. It's soaked," Katie complained.

That evening, as they sat down to eat tea together, everyone was unhappy. Goldie was barking next door because she wasn't allowed in the kitchen while they were eating, and Katie and Tom weren't even talking to each other after Katie had run off with Goldie to the park without asking Tom.

"That's it. I've had enough!" sighed their mum. "Unless you two make up and shape up, I'm afraid I'm going to have to talk to John about taking Goldie back," Sue warned them.

Katie and Tom looked at each other, horrified, and even Goldie stopped barking, as though she knew what was going on.

That night, Tom and Katie had a secret meeting after lights-out. "Tom," whispered Katie, "we've got to do something. This is getting serious now, Mum was really cross. Plus I hate it when we argue, and I'd die if we lost Goldie," she said.

"I've been thinking that, too," replied Tom. "We're just going to have to be much more strict from now on. Agreed?" he asked, seriously. "Agreed," nodded Katie.

A couple of weeks later, everything was going really well. Goldie, Katie, Tom and their mum had settled into a routine that was working. There were fewer muddy paws, fewer arguments, and fewer incidents in general. What's more, Goldie really did seem to be trying to behave herself, as well.

When John came round to check up on them, he was genuinely surprised at how well they all seemed to be doing.

"I have to say, I had a few doubts in my mind at first. Goldie's a very special lady, but

she is a pretty demanding one, too," he told them.

"Don't we know it!" laughed Sue, looking at her children. She explained about all the teething problems they had had at first, but how gradually they had managed to work things out between them.

"We wouldn't swap Goldie for anything in the world," said Katie, wrapping her arms around Goldie's neck. "Yeah," joked Tom as Goldie gave his hand a huge, sloppy lick. "Adopting a pet really is a *golden* opportunity!" he laughed. 🐾

MEMORY CHECK!

Find out how much you remember from the story with these teasers! Circle T for true or F for false.

1 Tom and Katie went to the library to find out all about dogs and dog breeds. T F

2 Katie and Tom wanted a puppy. T F

3 The lady who helped them fill out the forms at the RSPCA centre was called Natasha. T F

4 Katie and Tom were allowed to take Goldie home without having a home visit. T F

5 Goldie was a Labrador cross. T F

6 Katie and Tom had trouble commanding Goldie to 'Heel'. T F

7 The folder contained information about having Goldie neutered. T F

Answers: 1, true; 2, false; 3, false; 4, flase; 5, true; 6, true; 7, false.

Fill in this form all about your pet. If you don't have one, just describe what your ideal pet would be like! If you have lots of pets, choose one to write about here – you could make more files yourself if you like.

PET FILE

What's your pet's name?

What type of animal is he or she?

Where and when did you get your pet?

How old is he or she?

What's your first memory of your pet?

What's the best thing about your pet?

Tell a funny story about your pet:

Horses

Which horse can you spread with butter and jam?

Any purebread!

Pet care

● Horses have a life span of 20-25 years (though it can be 30 or more), so owning a horse means hard and mucky work every day for a long time.

● Hay there! Horses are strict herbivores and need a varied, balanced diet including: roughage (from hay), roots and fruits, a salt lick or mineral block, concentrates (as general feeds or in cube form) plus drinking water available at all times.

● A stabled horse needs daily exercise to keep it healthy. Try to turn it out to grass for a while each day so it can exercise itself naturally, and riding a pony daily is good exercise for you both!

● Horses are smart herd animals and so get bored easily and enjoy company. Try to exercise your pony with other horses as well as alone.

● With lots of daily care and equipment plus vet bills and shoeing, the costs do add up. But most owners agree, ponies are worth it.

What do ghosts like about riding horses?

Ghoulloping!

Amazing facts!

● The height of horses and ponies (horses measure 14.2 hands or over, ponies are 14.2 and under) is measured in hands and is the distance between the ground and the highest point of the horse's withers (top of the shoulders). Each hand equals about 8.5cm. If someone says a horse is 16 hands high, it's 1m 36cm tall!

● The world's smallest horse is 'Tara Stables Hope For Tomorrow' or 'Hope', for short! Hope is all

black, with a dark mane and tail. She belongs to the Miniature breed (no surprises there!) and in June 1997 measured 53.34cm from the ground to the highest point of the withers.

● The world's largest horse was a purebred Belgian stallion called Brooklyn Supreme who stood 19.2 hands (1.98m) at his withers. Foaled in 1928, Brooklyn died in 1948 and is in the Guinness Book of World Records.

Working with ANIMALS

VET

Becoming a vet takes a lot of hard study and time. You need to get the best grades while you are still at school and then spend at least five years at university to graduate with a degree in veterinary science. Adam Tjolle says he knew he wanted to be a vet when he was seven! There's lots of competition to get a place at university – as many as ten people applying for every place – and the workload can be tough. You have to treat all kinds of animals (not just fluffy ones), make difficult decisions and cope with suffering and sadness. But it's fascinating work and very rewarding, particularly when you manage to help an animal on the road to recovery – as we saw with little Bonnie

SO YOU THINK YOU'VE GOT WHAT IT TAKES TO WORK WITH ANIMALS? HERE ARE JUST SOME OF THE RSPCA STAFF WHO'VE APPEARED ON ANIMAL HOSPITAL WITH INFO ON HOW TO GET A JOB LIKE THEIRS!

here, who had damaged the nerves in one of her hind legs in an accident.

VETERINARY NURSE

Veterinary nurses assist veterinary surgeons during surgery, administer first aid, and carry out laboratory work and general ward care. They also feed and clean animals, write progress reports and do telephone and reception work. The two-year training period involves classroom tuition and practical experience.

To be a veterinary nurse, you need to be aged 17 or over and have at least four GCSEs with grades A to C including English and Maths.

The RSPCA employs some veterinary nurses, but most opportunities are in private practices.

RSPCA INSPECTOR

Most of the work of an RSPCA Inspector is responding to calls about animal cruelty. What you see can be quite upsetting – and usually quite infuriating, as Inspector Lee Hopgood made plain when he went to inspect an electrical shop in London where goldfish were being sold in unsuitable jars and bottles. Apart from being far too small, the jars had very narrow necks so little oxygen could get to the fish and they were in danger of dying. Back at the RSPCA Putney Hospital, the fish were released into a far more suitable aquarium.

Finding a new home for animals or releasing them makes the job seem very worthwhile, but it takes practice to get it right. The training to become an RSPCA Inspector involves six months of studying and working with trained inspectors. You have to be aged over 22 to start, have GCSEs in English and a science, and you must hold a driving licence and be able to swim. You

also need to have lots of experience working with people and animals and be very determined – the RSPCA receives hundreds of applications for every place.

RSPCA ANIMAL COLLECTION OFFICER

Patience and the ability to be prepared for anything are just two of the qualities you'll need to be an Animal Collection Officer, as Mark Hallam showed when he was called out to rescue this fox that had slipped down into a walled-off basement. Mark had to use his initiative to ensure a safe rescue – he needed to find a long ladder to reach down into the basement and ask a volunteer to help him get the frightened fox into the basket.

To become an Animal Collection Officer, you'll need a valid driving licence with at least

three years' driving experience. You'll also need to be in good physical shape and have some previous experience of working with animals.

If you can tick these boxes, you're the kind of person who could work with animals!

I love animals ☐

I like people as well ☐

I can get good results at school ☐

I am patient ☐

I don't mind working hard ☐

I can be gentle and strong, too ☐

GOOD GRIP!

'He's certainly got a good grip!' said Rolf when this 3-metre snake took a hold of his arm in the surgery at RSPCA Animal Hospital Putney. The snake had come in because its owner was concerned it had skin rot. Nothing a bit of iodine rubbed under the scales couldn't cure, explained the vet Adam Tjolle as he lifted up the scales to rub some in. But was the snake a boy or girl? 'It's easier to tell when there is a boy and girl snake next to each other – male snakes have longer tails,' said Adam. And judging by the length of the snake wrapped round Rolf's arm, this one was probably a boy!

Exotic animals rarely make suitable pets. They need careful treatment when something goes wrong. Here are some exotic pets that the Animal Hospital team encountered.

Unusual animals

SALA-MENDER

A salamander is a tropical amphibian, normally found abroad, so when an RSPCA inspector was contacted by a lady who had found an injured one in her back garden, it was obvious to the inspector that it had to be an escaped pet. Back at the RSPCA's Harmsworth Hospital, vet Gabriel Haggard inspected the salamander. Its back legs were injured and it had puncture wounds on either side of its pelvis. Gabriel said it had probably been attacked by a puzzled cat or dog. He used a syringe to spray antibiotics directly onto the wounds – instead of injecting them, which might have damaged the animal's delicate skin.

OUCH!

Sausages and bacon may be some people's idea of a slap-up breakfast, but are they any good for piranhas? The owner of two piranhas called Ronnie and Reggie had been given them by a friend and wasn't sure if they were the meat-eating kind or not. What he did know, though, was that the fish were too big for him to cope with, and he was relieved when RSPCA Chief Inspector Ian Gough found a new home for them at an animal sanctuary. The fish were so big that they had to be transported there in separate dustbins, each piranha safely inside in a strong plastic bag filled with water. Keeping his hands well out of the way, Ian helped release them into their new tanks. Yes, the carer confirmed, they were meat-eating, red-bellied piranhas – Ian's precautions had not been in vain!

EYE EYE EYE

When the owner of this iguana called Elmo brought him in to the hospital, she didn't expect to find out he had three eyes. But as vet Malcolm Paul explained, all iguanas have a 'third eye' – it's a small opening on top of their head that acts like a body clock. When the third eye is covered up, as if in darkness, the body naturally thinks it's time to sleep and so the iguana relaxes. This is worth knowing when you're trying to examine one, as Malcolm showed! Elmo's owner had been worried her pet was putting on too much weight. 'Not at all,' said Malcolm, 'Baby iguanas grow very quickly.' Malcolm then explained that as long as he kept on shedding his skin, Elmo was just a healthy one-year-old with lots of growing still to do!

Birds

What do you call a missing parrot? A polygon!

Pet care

● Budgies and canaries are great pets but really do depend on their owners to provide the daily care and attention necessary for their wellbeing.

● For extra vitamins and minerals, supplement seed mix with fruits, green foods and cuttlefish.

● In the wild, budgies travel in large flocks, so budgies should be kept in pairs for company and preferably be housed in a well-built aviary where they can move fairly freely and enjoy some flight.

● All bird cages should be put in a well-lit room that is not draughty and where the bird will have frequent human contact. It should also be a safe place for the bird to be released and exercised in.

● Be careful not to fasten your birds' water or food containers under any perches, as droppings could accidentally contaminate their contents.

● NB! The RSPCA advises against keeping any bird that has not been bred in captivity.

Amazing facts!

● The domestic budgie has been bred from the wild budgerigar *Melopsittacus undulatus* and is now the world's most popular species of pet bird.

● The average budgie weighs only 2 grams at birth, growing to 30-35 grams and 19cm tall as an adult.

● The most famous budgie is probably Sparkie Williams. He knew over 550 words, eight nursery rhymes, 360 phrases, he appeared on radio shows and even sold 20,000 copies of his own record!

● There are 358 species of parrot, which include cockatoos, lovebirds, lorikeets – and budgies! Depending on the speicies, parrots in captivity can live for 40 to over 100 years!

● Male budgies have a blue waxy cere around their nostrils and females have a brown one.

FULL OF STONES

When Cindy didn't seem to be reacting to antibiotic treatment for a suspected urinary infection, vet Bairbre O'Malley thought the problem could be worse and suspected it may be a tumour in her bladder. However, an x-ray showed that it wasn't a tumour but a huge bladder stone. It needed to be removed immediately so Cindy was anaesthetised and, two hours later, Bairbre managed to remove the stone. It was very big – the size of a ping pong ball. Bairbre was amazed. After the big operation, Cindy had two weeks' rest at home before returning to the hospital to have her stitches removed. Bairbre was pleased with her recovery – Cindy was far bubblier and full of beans. Much better than being full of stones!

OUCH!

This dog, Cane, was brought into an RSPCA hospital when he lost his bark and started bringing his food up. Had he swallowed something, his owner wondered? The vet looked in Cane's mouth and could just see some cotton sewing thread that looked like it was stuck down his throat. She needed to find out if a needle was attached to it.

X-rays of his throat, chest and abdomen didn't show anything, but as Helen began to pull out the cotton, she had a nasty shock. There was a needle, stuck right into Cane's tongue. Very carefully, she pulled it out. Fortunately, Cane's tongue was not sore for too long.

Not much surprises the staff at the RSPCA Animal Hospitals – with years of experience, they've often seen it all before. But for things that end up in animals' stomachs, these dogs really take the biscuit!

COLLARED!

The X-ray was all too clear – pit bull terrier Reggie really had eaten his own collar. 'I went out yesterday for an hour and when I came home he'd eaten his collar,' said owner Jo Darcey. 'He was just sitting in his bed, looking at me rather guiltily,' she added, confessing that Reggie had been known to eat kitchen tiles and even bricks in the past! Although RSPCA Putney Veterinary Director Tessa Bailey could see Reggie looked quite bright and chirpy, she was concerned that the metal studs in the collar could damage him or cause an obstruction as they passed through his system. They decided to make Reggie sick. Some studs did come up, but Tessa felt it was still necessary to operate. Just as well, as she discovered seven more studs and a couple of bits of collar still in Reggie's stomach. A few days later, Reggie (and his unusual appetite) was back to normal – although Tessa suggested that when they next went out the owners should leave Reggie with something that smelled of them (for instance sheets or towels) so he didn't get quite so frantic.

BARNIE'S BONE

This cuddly sheepdog called Barnie had eaten a polystyrene tray that had contained meat. Although Barnie didn't seem in pain, he hadn't been sick so the tray was obviously still inside. Vet Jeremy Stewart felt Barnie's stomach and abdomen and said the dog's tummy felt a 'bit gassy,' which suggested a problem. An X-ray showed he needed to operate – and when he did, he found some large, sharp pieces of bone which had to be removed. The operation was a success, as vet Jeremy was able to remove the polystyrene *and* the pieces of bone. Ten days later, Barnie came back to have his stitches removed. Everyone was pleased to see he had made a full recovery but Jeremy warned Barnie's owners that dogs should never be allowed cooked bones, and should only be allowed raw bones rarely.

Every year, the RSPCA receives over 1.6 million calls for information and assistance. Here are some typical questions - and the replies

Q. I've seen a fox in my garden. Can foxes be dangerous?

Foxes are generally fearful of people and will try to avoid adults and children. Sometimes, though, bolder foxes will go into gardens in broad daylight – looking for a quiet place to rest, foraging for food scraps, or just being inquisitive. Their boldness is not a sign of aggression – a healthy fox would only attack a person if provoked. Many people love to watch foxes from a distance in their garden. But it is important to remember that foxes are wild animals, which may carry disease, and that you should not try to touch them or tame them.

If you want to feed foxes, they will eat meat in almost any form – cooked or raw – as well as cooked vegetables. You should provide enough food for only one meal, otherwise leftovers may go off and cause sickness or attract unwanted visitors.

Q. If I see an animal being cruelly treated, who should I call and what would I need to say?

You could call the RSPCA's 24-hour cruelty hotline on 0870 55 55 999, or the police. You would need to give a description of the animal involved, the precise location of the animal, the names and addresses of other witnesses, the registration number of any vehicle involved, and the name and address of the suspect(s) if known. The Society relies on voluntary donations so its resources are far more limited than the police or other emergency services. Although the RSPCA can be contacted at any time of the day or night, RSPCA inspectors can only attend calls outside normal office hours (9am-5pm, Monday to Friday) in an emergency. The Society will always do its best to help an animal in need, but it can only act within the law and, although the RSPCA is constantly campaigning for improvements to animal welfare laws, sadly there are sometimes no laws to protect the animals involved.

Q. I've lost my dog, what should I do?

Contact your regional office of the RSPCA on 0870 55 55 999 to provide details for their lost and found register.

If someone finds your dog and contacts the regional office, the RSPCA will then have the relevant information needed to try and reunite you.

Other organisations that keep records of lost and found animals are: Pet Search, tel: 01225 705175; the National Canine Defence League, tel: 020 7837 0006 and Pet Match, tel: 0870 1600 999.

Get in touch with the dog warden via your local council, local veterinary surgeries, animal centres and the police. Your milkman and postman may also be able to look out for your pet on their rounds.

Put up posters in the area with a picture of your pet and your contact details. You could also put details up in newsagents, schools and newspapers. Local radio stations might even be happy to make an announcement about your search.

But the best way to make your search easier is to make sure that your pet is microchipped in the first place.

Q. My pet died and I am so upset. How can I come to terms with his death?

It is natural to feel sad and upset. Your pet was probably part of your life for a long time; you have looked after it, fed it, loved it and enjoyed its company. Give yourself time to get over the loss. Some people feel better after a few weeks, but others find that remembering their pet's death makes them upset or even angry for a long time after.

These emotions are part of the process of coming to terms with your loss.

It may help to talk about your animal's death, especially to friends and relatives who have had a similar experience. Some people also find it helps to write their feelings down in a diary or maybe a poem. You could hold a special remembrance ceremony – bury a memento or plant a tree in a favourite part of the garden.

And don't forget to remember the good times you had together, too. Think about your pet's funny habits and what you loved most about it, and hopefully you will soon be able to remember your pet with a smile.

Q. What should you do if you find a baby bird away from its mother and its nest?

If it is not injured or in an exposed area, it's best to leave the baby bird alone. Fledglings (the proper name for baby birds) often leave the nest before they are ready to fly and in most cases are perfectly fine. Their parents are usually watching and waiting nearby and will keep feeding them. If the fledgling is in an open place that is not safe, you could try to encourage it to a safe area where its parents can find it.

But, if you think the bird may be injured, or you find a nestling – an unfeathered young bird – which has fallen out of its nest, then please call the RSPCA on 0870 55 55 999 for advice. Never try to put a nestling back in its nest on your own in case you disturb the other birds, and never try to look after a young bird yourself – it will need expert attention if it is to survive.

To find out more about the work the RSPCA does, look at their website at www.rspca.org.uk or write to them at Enquiries Service, RSPCA, Wilberforce Way, Southwater, Horsham, West Sussex RH13 7WN.

Cats

Pet care

● The independent but loving nature of domestic cats makes them fairly easy pets to keep, and a cat can live for 14-20 years if looked after properly by its owner.

● Cats are considered clean pets as they take great care in their own grooming. However, long-haired breeds will need help with this on a daily basis, and even short-haired varieties may need gentle combing and brushing during moulting. This is especially important as cats can choke on fur balls (hair that gets lodged in their throats during cleaning).

● Cats don't have many basic requirements, but they do need a warm and safe place to sleep – whether it be a comfy chair, basket or lined box – particularly as they spend so much time napping! The RSPCA also recommends that you try to keep your cat indoors at night. This is the time when most cat fights and cat-related road traffic accidents occur.

● Cats tend to become fussy eaters, so they need to be taught to accept a variety of foods from an early age. A cat's diet should be high in protein and fat, and they should be fed little and often. Most tinned cat food is specially made with extra vitamins and minerals. It can be occasionally accompanied by some dried cat biscuits for extra variety, but always make sure there is plenty of clean, fresh water available.

● Even the fussiest, cleanest cats and kittens need de-fleaing and worming regularly with special preparations. Always ask a vet about which preparations are most suitable for your cat, and don't forget to de-flea the cat's bedding and usual environment, too (see page 53 for more details)!

● All cats need to be able to exercise, whether indoors or out. If a cat doesn't have ready access to a garden, keep an extra close eye on their claws and your furniture! It's a good idea to provide a scratching post to save your furniture from being shredded and their claws from becoming overgrown and painful.

● Owners can understand their cats better by being watchful of their body language (as well as listening to the miaows)! Raised fur or a flicking tail can indicate an unhappy or scared cat, and most owners agree that purring is the best sound a cat can make.

What did one cat say to another?

You're purrfect!

41

Cats

What did the cat say when he lost all his money?
I'm paw!

Cat napping

Cat burglar

Cat's cradle

When the cat's away, the mice will play!

Cat and mouse

You look like the cat that got the cream!

The cat has nine lives!

Cat on hot bricks!

Amazing facts!

● A cat can fit through any tiny gap or opening that is the size of its head. This is because, unlike humans, cats do not have a collarbone.

● The cat's ear contains around 30 muscles (we humans only have six), which is how a cat can rotate its ears through 180 degrees. Cats can also turn in the direction of a sound about ten times faster than even the best watchdog.

● Cats spend up to 18 hours out of every 24 sleeping, but only a third of this is deep sleep. Cats are hunters so even when they are in a deep sleep they are on standby to defend territory and protect themselves.

● The oldest reliably-documented cat was a female tabby called Ma. Ma was put to sleep at the grand age of 34, on 5 November, 1957.

● The most pricey cat was Cato who, in February 1990, was sold for £25,000 to Cindy Jackson in London. As a second generation Bengal, Cato is a wildcat hybrid (resulting from breeding a domestic cat with a wild Asian leopard cat). Apparently, Cato occasionally wears an 18-carat gold and diamond Cartier necklace when attending his owner's parties!

● A cat has 24 whiskers – four rows on each side – which it uses for measuring distances. The slightest touch on a cat's whiskers will make its eyes blink.

● On 21 November 1997, Snowbie, an affectionate white cat, entered the Guinness Book of Records for being the longest cat. Aged four, Snowbie measured a whopping 103cm from his nose to the tip of his tail!

Draw a cat

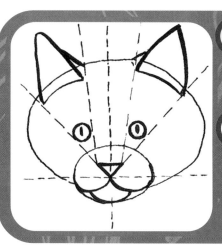

1 Use a photo for reference if you can – it won't move about like a pet does!

2 Start with a pencil sketch of shapes. Our cat has two squashed circles for its head and muzzle and a triangle for a nose.

3 Draw guidelines going out from the nose to help position your cat's eyes and ears.

4 Add the mouth, then rub out the guidelines and soften the edges.

5 Then bring your cat to life with colour!

Sketch the rest of this cat's markings, then colour it in using pencils or felt-tips.

43

PUZZLES

Have you got what it takes to solve these puzzles? See page 58 to chec

Some days at the Animal Hospital are pretty chaotic, and this looks like one of them! Can you spot the differences between these two scenes? There are ten to find.

Secret message!

Use the letters you've been given to help fill in the rest of the alphabet code. Then use it to finish the rhyming pet and vet message.

1	2	3	4	5	6	7	8	9	10	11	12	13	14	15	16	17	18	19	20	21	22	23	24	25	26
W		Y		A	B	C	D	E	f	g	h	I	J	K	L	M	N	O	P		R	S		U	V

13 10	3 19 25	12 5 26 9	5	20 19 19 22 16 3
I F	Y O U	H A V E	A	P O O R L Y

20 9 24	3 19 25	17 25 23 24	24 5 15 9	13 24
P E T	Y O U	M U S T	T A K E	I T

24 19	24 12 9	26 9 24	7 22 25 9 16 24 3
T O	T h e	V E T	C R U E L T Y

1 19 22 22 13 9 23	18 13 11 12 24	19 22	8 5 3
W O R R I e s,	N i g h T	O R	d a y?

14 25 23 24	7 5 16 16	24 12 9	22 23 20 7 5
J U S T	C A L L	T H E	R S P C A.

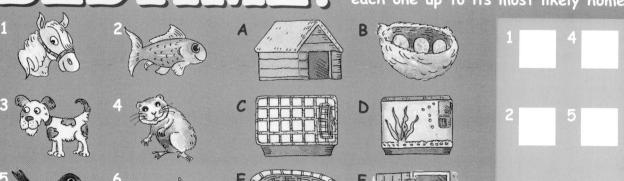

BEDTIME!

Put the animals to bed by matching each one up to its most likely home.

1 2 3 4 5 6

A B C D E F

1		4	
2		5	
3		6	

45

All in a day's work

Follow a day with vet Julie Taylor at the RSPCA Animal Hospital in Putney.

1 It's Saturday morning Emergency Surgery. The first casualty vet Julie Taylor sees is Tahur the tabby, who had been hit by a car. Julie examines Tahur and discovers his tail has been hurt.

2 Tahur isn't too bad. He's walking around happily and still eating. Julie puts him on antibiotic tablets and tells his owners that they will need to bathe his tail in salt water daily.

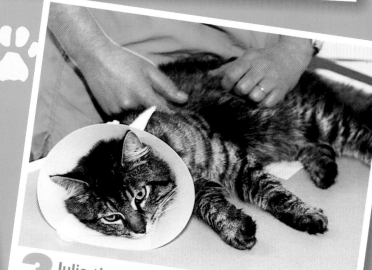

3 Julie then puts a lampshade collar on Tahur so that he can't lick his tail and make it sore. But Tahur doesn't seem to mind.

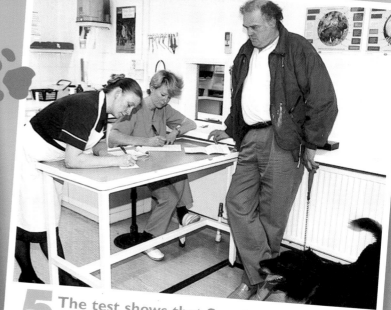

4 Next in is Scooby, who's 15 years old. He's been drinking a lot and losing weight. Julie examines him, checks his tummy and takes a drop of blood for testing.

5 The test shows that Scooby is diabetic. This means he will need insulin injections every day. Scooby will have to stay at the hospital until the team can work out how much insulin he will need.

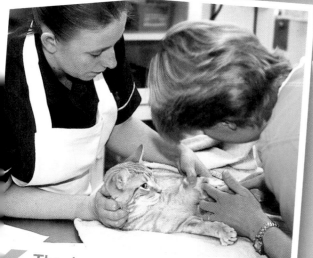

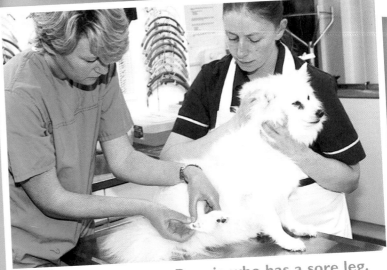

6 The day gets busier as Julie and nurse Lisa take an x-ray of a cat called Benjamin, who was hit by a car, see if he has any broken bones.

7 Then they treat Bonnie who has a sore leg. She has an anaesthetic so they can check some pins in her leg that were put in a while ago but have now started to trouble her.

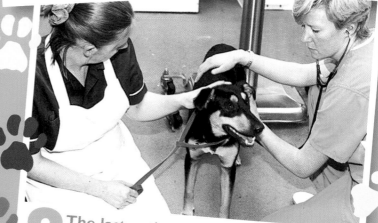

8 It's nearly the end of the day and there's just time to check on Tom. He had gone missing and returned home limping, but he's much better now.

9 The last patient is Zoe, who came in at 3am after being hit by a car. Julie was on night duty so she was there when Zoe came in. Zoe is still a bit nervous so Julie makes a fuss of her. What a busy day!

47

Hamsters

Where do hamsters come from? Hamsterdam!

Pet care

● Hamsters have an average lifespan of only two to three years so it is important to buy young hamsters, aged from four to eight weeks.

● Hamsters do *not* enjoy the company of other hamsters! So if you keep more than one, you'll need separate cages – or the hamsters may well fight and could seriously hurt or kill each other.

● The more space you can give your hamster, the better. Some of the more expensive homes are multi-level cages with interconnecting tubes and areas. These look fun, but adult Golden hamsters may grow too big to go through the tubes!

● Hamsters should be fed each evening on balanced, dry hamster mix, bought from pet shops. Your hamster will also enjoy occasional healthy treats such as small amounts of fruit and veg.

● Hamsters enjoy making friends with and being handled by their owners, as long as they're gentle! Sudden moves or noises easily frighten them.

Amazing facts!

● The Syrian or Golden hamster is the UK's most popular small pet. On average it is 15-20cms long.

● In 1974, a pet hamster litter of an incredible 26 young was recorded – the average is eight!

● Dwarf hamsters are believed to communicate with each other using tiny ultrasonic squeaks that can't be heard by the human ear!

● Hamsters are rodents which means they have large incisor teeth that are continually growing. This means they need to gnaw to prevent their teeth overgrowing. (Brazil nuts are great for this!)

● Hamsters have expandable cheek pouches where they can carry food and bedding back to their burrow in the wild, and where they can store food. The word hamster comes from the German word 'hamstern', which means 'to hoard'.

PUZZLES

Spot the animal

We've zoomed in on some animals. Can you guess what they are?

1

2

4

3

5

WORDSEARCH

Look up, down, diagonally and across to find the pet care words in the list. How many can you get?

```
Y W T X G Q D T X C B C M V J Z L W A F
A L J F Q H G Z W P G Y I K N S H C R L
J R A A S W O Y F T T I S Z S H K L O C
V K S U D P N C C R D V F G M V F O Q B
C J R P U Q R L E C F N K I G G G W E X
Z B C A Q T E T M E O D G X U H M M N X
I U X A L A A P V J O W B V R A O L I X
T R W Q N W W O C T D I U R F P U O H R
T A W A S H L N R Y Y F V E L U A R W S
D C E Y W M C B M E O R J T S A G W J T
Z V Y Q K L R H S Z X S P L A L G E J M
C O V I H T Q I F E Y E R E R N C D B V
O C P B H A C B E G E U O H Z K G S F F
H H A S H R W Y H L U F M S Z P S T E W
W T C I E X L M S L O R Z I F P K X I V
V L Q X Z O Y H P R A U U T H B O P M R
A A E F H U U S B W V L A S F Y E Y U T
D E V I Z R O Y M A P H J C O Y V A U R
W H N G X E W P Q G K B E D D I N G Z M
X V G S B O S D L G D K C T X B N P W H
```

FOOD
WATER
EXERCISE
SLEEP
LOVE
WARM
WASH
SHELTER
BRUSH
GROOM
CLEAN
SHINE
HEALTH
BEDDING

What is the best kind of computer bug?

Spiders – because they make the best "web" sites (geddit?)

What do you call a seagull when it flies over a bay?

A bagel!

What do you get when you cross a rhinoceros with a blackbird?

A lot of broken telephone poles!

50

Animal crossword

How well do you know your animals? Try this to see! If you get stuck, reread the pages on caring for pets.

ACROSS

1 Royal Society for the Prevention of Cruelty to Animals (abbr.)
3 Man's best friend?
6 This pet bird just won't budge from the No 1 popularity spot!
8 This exotic pet might make your bones rattle!
10 Syrian or Golden ones are the most popular in the UK.
13 Taller than a pony?
14 Male deer
15 Baaaa!

DOWN

1 Bugs Bunny?
2 Just like humans wear shoes, dogs and cats have some of these to protect their paws!
3 Your dog might do this to find his buried bone!
4 Unmuddle BRELGI to get this furry pet out of a spin!
5 This clear drink is essential stuff for all thirsty pets!
7 It's not all black and white for this piggy rodent!
9 What all animals do with food
11 Zzzzzzzz!
12 Made of gold? Unlikely... how would it float?

ANIMAZE! Which pet finds their way to Rolf?

TURN TO PAGE 58 FOR THE ANSWERS! ➔

ASK A VET

SOME COMMON PROBLEMS WITH POPULAR PETS

Tessa Bailey, veterinary director at the RSPCA Animal Hospital Putney, answers your pet problems!

Feather Duster?!

Q. My budgie keeps plucking out her own feathers. What does this mean? We have recently moved house so I wonder if it could be linked to that?

Feather plucking is often a symptom of boredom or stress, which may well have been brought on by your house move.

To try to prevent this habit from developing you need to administer some TLC (tender loving care)! Increasing the amount of stimulation (from toys, talking and exercise) and company it gets may well do the trick.

If the condition does not improve, you should seek advice from your vet, who may prescribe a special collar to prevent it from plucking itself any more.

Worm Worries!

Q. How can you tell if your cat or dog has worms? Do any other animals get worms?

Most animals (including humans!) can get worms, but nearly all dogs and cats come into contact with worms and so get tapeworms or roundworms at some point in their lives.

Even animals which look in tip-top condition and don't show signs of ill health can carry them, which means it can be difficult to diagnose. So it's important to worm your animals regularly – not just for their sakes, but for yours, as some types can be dangerous to human health.

Signs that unwelcome wormy visitors have arrived include weight loss and a coarse or harsh (out of condition) coat and a swollen and sore tummy. An infected dog or cat may drag itself about on its rear or lick its bottom more than usual, too.

If you see any worms on your animal (they tend to be most obvious in vomit or faeces – but do NOT touch them with bare hands!), carefully wrap them up in damp cotton wool and take them to the vet, who will be able to treat the animal.

Puffy Pouch!

Q. One of my hamster's cheek pouches looks bigger than the other and he doesn't seem to be eating on that side.

Your hamster may have an abscess in its cheek. This can happen if a hamster tries to store too much food in its mouth. If the food start to rot, it can cause an infection which would make the cheek swell. Yo might also notice a discharge from the infected area.

Another cause might be teeth problems, such as an overgrown incisc scratching the inside of your hamster's mouth. Take your hamster to the vet to be examined and treated immediately.

lea the Scenery!

. How can I check my cat for fleas, and how ould I get rid of them? I have some insect bites n my arm and my cat has been scratching a lot.

cratching could be a sign of fleas. Other signs are small rown/black insects scurrying about (often quite difficult o see) or tiny brown or black specks in your kitten's fur probably flea droppings). To check, put a damp piece of white kitchen roll underneath your cat and rub its fur briskly. Any flea dirt falling onto the paper will dissolve nto a brownish red smudge.

Even the cleanest cats in the best-kept homes can get fleas, but they can be controlled. The fleas and eggs are often found in the animal's bedding. Your vet will recommend products. Regularly cleaning the bedding and vacuuming furniture and floors helps to destroy each stage of the flea's life cycle. Throw away the dustbag after each use to prevent eggs and larvae developing.

Home for a hedgehog?

Q. What should I do if I find a hedgehog in winter?

Trying to overwinter a hedgehog in winter that is not hibernating is really a job for the experts. If you see a hedgehog that looks injured or orphaned, check first that it hasn't been recently disturbed from its nest or that its mother isn't watching from a distance. If you still think the hedgehog needs help, call the RSPCA or ask an adult to take it to a nearby vet or animal rescue centre. The rescue centre will weigh the orphaned hedgehog to check if it needs overwintering – an injured or baby hedgehog weighing less than about 450g will need their help. If you do want to leave out food for hedgehogs in the colder months, you should leave water, tinned pet food (that is not fish-based), insects, worms and some dried biscuits or bread. It is not

a good idea to leave out just bread and milk (as many people believe), because this can give hedgehogs diarrhoea and doesn't provide them with all the necessary nutrients to keep them healthy.

Poorly Pony!

Q. We have recently moved our horse into a new field and she seems to have been unwell with colic. What should we do?

Colic is a digestive problem that can be caused by poor feeding, worm infection, impacted intestines or a sudden change in diet – which may have been the cause of your pony's problem.

The symptoms of colic include sweating and a raised temperature (above 39 degrees) and severe tummy pain, which may make your pony twist round to look at or try to kick its tummy or flank. The pony may even lie down or try to roll on its tummy to relieve the pain.

If you think your pony is suffering from colic, you should remove all food and water – which means taking it out of its field and stabling it. You should increase its bedding to prevent injury, and if the pony seems restless, walk it around gently.

Do not let your pony lie down. If the symptoms last longer than an hour or are very severe, call your vet. Fortunately, surgery is rarely necessary.

Gerbils and mice

Pet care

● Gerbils and mice have an average lifespan of two to three years, and enjoy the company of others of their own sex, kind and family.

● Gerbils and mice need a daily diet of mixed grain and washed fruit and vegetables (mice also need a salt lick) and they both need fresh water from a drip-feed bottle with a metal spout.

● Pet gerbils and mice need a gnawing block of smooth wood or a piece of fruit tree branch to wear down their long teeth.

● Old food should be removed daily from the gerbilarium, which needs a thorough clean every three months. The gerbilarium needs to contain plenty of material for burrowing (slightly damp peat mixed with straw is ideal). Toys, like cardboard tubes and wooden cotton reels, will help your gerbil exercise.

● A mouse's bedding must be changed at least once a week. Its home should also have a solid exercise wheel, hiding places and climbing ropes.

What do mice do when they're at home?

Mousework!

Amazing facts!

● Most domestic gerbils are relatives of the Mongolian gerbil (*Meriones unguiculatus*), which originated in north-eastern China.

● In the wild, gerbils live in underground groups called colonies. Their underground homes have tunnels, sometimes two or three metres long.

● Domesticated mice descend from the house mouse. House mice originated in Asia, but nowadays mice are the most widely distributed mammals on Earth (apart from humans).

● Gerbils have around four to six young in each litter, whereas mice tend to have larger litters of six to fourteen babies!

● The earliest domesticated mice were kept as pets in the royal palaces of Japanese and Chinese emperors.

Dear Animal Hospital...

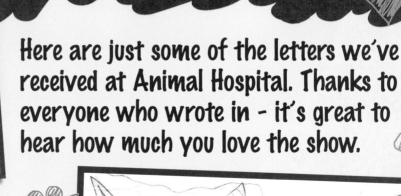

Here are just some of the letters we've received at Animal Hospital. Thanks to everyone who wrote in - it's great to hear how much you love the show.

This goldfish is by **Fiona Campbell** from Ross-shire. Fiona was doing a class project about caring for pets. Well done, Fiona!

'I want to be a vet when I grow up,' says **Connie McKay** from Scotland who has a puppy called Ebony and two guinea pigs called Bubbles and Cuddles.

All we need is a loving home and a caring one too thanks.

Help RSPCA by buying and re-homing a dog or cat or any animal please.

Good work, **Alice Reid**. Alice is 7. 'Me and my dog Jim watch your show every time it's on,' she says. 'And my fish thinks it's great, too.'

ANIMALS

What fantastic pets! They're by Kayleigh Packer who wants to be an RSPCA Inspector when she grows up. She already helps out at a vet's surgery and an animal sanctuary called Faraway Countryside Park in Devon. Good luck, Kayleigh.

PS - turn back to pages 30-31 for more info on working with animals.

'I watch Rolf on telly every week. The animals are really sweet,' says Sophie Mahon who's 8 and drew this pic of Rolf. Not a bad likeness at all!

Dear Rolf Harris
I am 10 and I love animals. I watch Animal Hospital whenever I can. I have a cat called Mucky, another cat called Aeris and a rabbit called Forest. My mum says I have a special bond with cats. Is it true that cats can tell when you love them? Most of our pets have been rescued. My favourite animal is the tiger because they're big and fierce!

Yours sincerely
Yasmin Harper

Dear Rolf Harris
I love your songs and your animals! I don't have one unfortunately. I would love one but I am not allowed to have one. My best song is Waltzing Matilda.

From Lisa Martin

Dear Rolf Harris
I really enjoy watching Animal Hospital. I love animals. I used to have a rabbit called Blacky but sadly it died. But it had a good life of 8 years.

From Leah Witham

The address for Animal Hospital fan mail is
Room 4604, White City, 201 Wood Lane, London W12 7TS

PROBLEMS SOLVED!

Puzzled out? Here are the answers to the puzzles on pages 12-13, 44-45 and 50-51.

Spot the animal

1 Fox
2 Dog
3 Cat
4 Horse
5 Hedgehog

WORDSEARCH

```
Y W T X G Q D T X C B C M V J Z L W A F
A L J F Q H G Z W P G Y I K N S H C R L
J R A A S W O Y F T T I S Z S H K L O C
V K S U D P N C C R D V F G M V F O O B
C J R P U Q R L E C F N K I G G G W E X
Z B C A Q T E T M E O D G X U H M M N X
I U X A L A A P V J O W B V R A O L I R
T R W Q N W W O C T D I U R F P O O H Z
T A W A S H L N R Y Y F V E L U R W S W
D C E Y W M C B M E O R J T S A G W J T
Z V Y Q K L R H S Z X S P L A L G E J M
C O V I H T Q I F E Y E R E R N C D B V
O C P B H A C B E G E U O H Z K G S F Y
H H A S H R W Y H L U F M S Z P S T E W
W T C I E X L M S L O R Z I F P K X I V
V L Q X Z O Y H P R A U U T H B O P M R
A A E F H U U S B W V L A S F Y E Y U T
D E V I Z R O Y M A P H J C O Y V A U R
W H N G X E W P Q G K B E D D I N G Z M
X V G S B O S D L G D K C T X B N P W H
```

Animal crossword

Across

1 RSPCA
3 Dog
6 Budgerigar
8 Snake
10 Hamster
13 Horse
14 Stag
15 Sheep

Down

1 Rabbit
2 Pad
3 Dig
4 Gerbil
5 Drink
7 Guinea pig
9 Eat
11 Sleep
12 Fish

ANIMAZE!

Answer = Cat

Woodland wildlife

There are 4 squirrels, 3 deer, 1 badger, 1 fox, 3 butterflies, 2 woodpeckers, 5 frogs, 1 newt, 2 hedgehogs, 1 dragonfly, 1 owl.

BEDTIME!

1 —F   4 —C
2 —D   5 —B
3 —A   6 —E

Secret message!

ANSWER = If you have a poorly pet, you must take it to the vet. Cruelty worries, night or day? Just call the RSPCA!

1	2	3	4	5	6	7	8	9	10	11	12	13	14	15	16	17	18	19	20	21	22	23	24	25	26
W	X	Y	Z	A	B	C	D	E	F	G	H	I	J	K	L	M	N	O	P	Q	R	S	T	U	V

HAPPY ENDING

Rhodri Williams tells the story of a stray cat who stole the show

Every series, there's at least one animal whose story really pulls at the viewers' heartstrings and last year, Shaun was definitely one of those. He'd been brought in as a stray and, with maggots climbing underneath him and his fur all matted, you could hardly tell he was a cat, let alone a Persian.

Drastic action was needed and RSPCA Putney Animal Hospital vet Adam Tjolle soon got to work shaving off his hair (complete with maggots). His new hair cut meant there was only one name for him: Shaun.

As he was a stray, Shaun needed a new home. And even though we're often saying how we can't deal with adoption queries at the programme (you should contact your local RSPCA Rescue Centre instead), lots of viewers wrote in offering him a home.

After a thorough search, the person who could offer him the time and patience that he needed was found. Samantha Blythe took him in and little by little, she encouraged Shaun to feel at home. 'He started behind the sofa and it was very hard to get to him,' she explained to us when we visited Shaun after a few weeks in his new home. 'But we've gradually moved him out. A couple of

times, he's even sat on the floor beside us. He likes being somewhere warm and getting lots of affection. It's taken him a while to get used to it, but hopefully this is the start of many Christmases for him.'

Shaun had already begun to trust Samantha enough to let her groom him. And as he sat by the Christmas tree, it looked like he had decided that this Christmas was just purrr-fect!

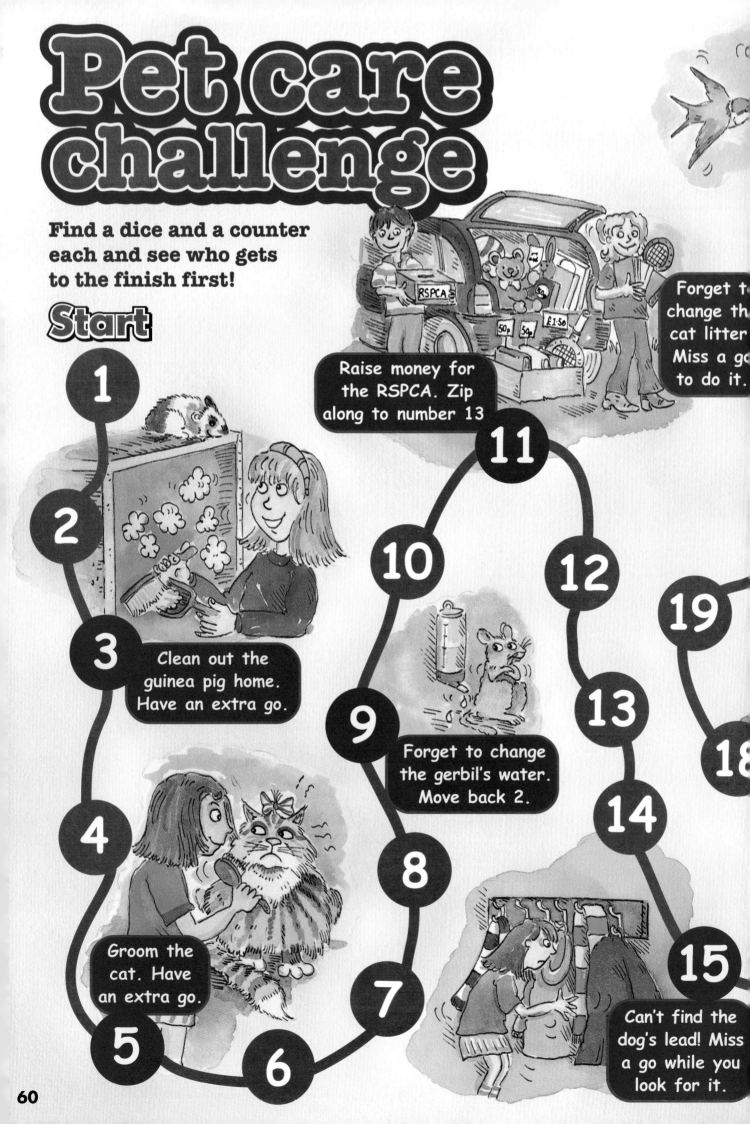

Pet care challenge

Find a dice and a counter each and see who gets to the finish first!

Start

1

2

3 Clean out the guinea pig home. Have an extra go.

4

Groom the cat. Have an extra go.

5

6

7

8

9 Forget to change the gerbil's water. Move back 2.

10

11 Raise money for the RSPCA. Zip along to number 13

12

13

14

15 Can't find the dog's lead! Miss a go while you look for it.

Forget to change the cat litter. Miss a go to do it.

19

18

60